Ice Creams and Space Dreams

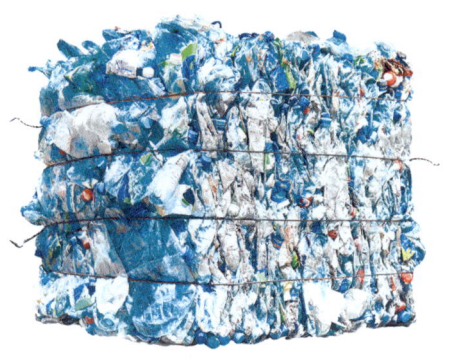

Contents

Chapter 1 Ice cream for all! 2
How did the machine work? 12
Chapter 2 The code-busting superstar 14
Hedy Lamarr, film star and inventor 26
Chapter 3 Bulletproof 28
Kevlar: wonder material 40
Chapter 4 Fighting disease 42
How does SAMBA work? 54
Chapter 5 Science is for everyone 56
3D films and experiences 66
Chapter 6 Turning trash into cash 68
Waste to plastic bricks 80
Timeline 82
Glossary 84
About the author 86
Book chat 88

Chapter 1
Ice cream for all!

Imagine looking out at the world and asking yourself: "What can I create today?" Inventors do just that – they think of useful or exciting ideas and figure out how to bring them to life.

Through history, many famous inventors were men. They included Alexander Graham Bell, who invented the telephone, and Thomas Edison, who thought up lots of things, including a type of light bulb.

Alexander Graham Bell

Thomas Edison

Until about 100 years ago, most women were expected to cook and clean at home. They weren't usually allowed to go to university or become experts in sciences or engineering. This situation changed slowly, and it made it hard for women to be inventors.

But a creative mind can't be silenced!

Inventor fact file

Nancy Johnson

Year of birth: 1795

Born in: New York, US

Invented: the first ice cream machine

Ice cream: a treat for the rich

People have eaten ice cream for hundreds of years – or even longer! There's evidence that Roman emperors enjoyed this treat as far back as 2,000 years ago.

The earliest ice cream wasn't very creamy. It was more like a sorbet made of snow and crushed berries.

A sorbet is made of fruit and sugar.

Ice cream includes milk or cream.

Through the years, the recipe for ice cream has changed. Milk or cream was added, making it thicker – more like the ice cream we eat today.

In the early 1800s, ice cream was a rare treat. It took hours to prepare. Modern freezers didn't exist, so there was no easy way of chilling the ingredients or keeping them cold. This meant that ice cream was a luxury food: only rich people with servants had the chance to enjoy it.

All that changed when Nancy Johnson invented the hand-cranked ice cream machine.

Nancy Johnson – born Nancy Donaldson – started life in New York and later moved to Pennsylvania, both in the US.

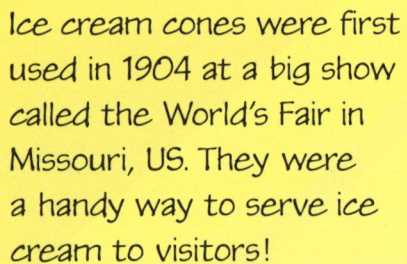

Ice cream cones were first used in 1904 at a big show called the World's Fair in Missouri, US. They were a handy way to serve ice cream to visitors!

During Nancy's lifetime, women had very few rights. For example, she was not allowed to vote, or to control her own money.

When Nancy got married in 1823, all her money became the property of her husband. But that didn't stop her from inventing an ice cream-making machine.

The outside of Nancy's ice cream machine was a wooden bucket that contained crushed ice. Inside, there was a metal cylinder where you put the ice cream ingredients. Once the lid was bolted onto the machine, a lever called a "crank" was used to spin a paddle inside the cylinder.

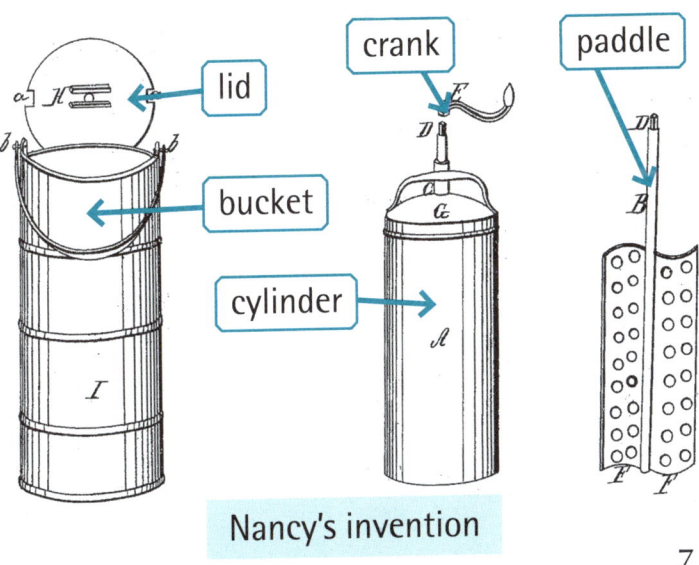

Nancy's invention

The ice cream revolution

New Zealanders eat more ice cream than people in any other country. They get through over 28 litres per person each year!

Before Nancy's invention, people usually made ice cream in a pot inside a bucket of crushed ice and salt. They had to stir the ingredients for hours to get them cold enough, and the results often came out lumpy.

Nancy's invention only took 30 minutes to make really smooth ice cream. For a fee, individuals, small shops and cafes could build their own ice cream machines based on her plans. As a result, more people could enjoy this much-loved treat.

Salt can lower the temperature of ice and stop it melting. That's why people used salt in ice cream makers.

children enjoying ice cream in a shop in 1955

The secret ingredient

Ice cream is made from things like milk, sugar, fruit and chocolate. But the secret ingredient is air! The perfect scoop of ice cream is whipped to fold air into the mixture. That's why there seems to be less ice cream when it melts!

Best eaten slowly

Because of Nancy's machine, more children discovered the pleasures of ice cream. Although it's best to eat it slowly ...

The science of brain freeze

Brain freeze is a short headache caused by eating cold food or drinks. It often happens if you eat quickly. When your body senses an extreme change in the temperature of your mouth, it sends extra blood to your head to warm you up. This rush of blood feels uncomfortable, but fortunately, the pain goes away quickly!

Nancy made 1,500 dollars from her invention, which is about 60,000 dollars in today's money. Lots of other people invented new ice cream machines, but hers was the first.

These days, most of the ice cream we eat comes from factories. It's over 150 years since Nancy invented her hand-cranked ice cream maker. Yet, amazingly, you can still buy similar machines and make your own ice cream at home.

Fruit, chocolate or sprinkles? What will you put in yours?

BONUS
How did the machine work?

ice cream machine

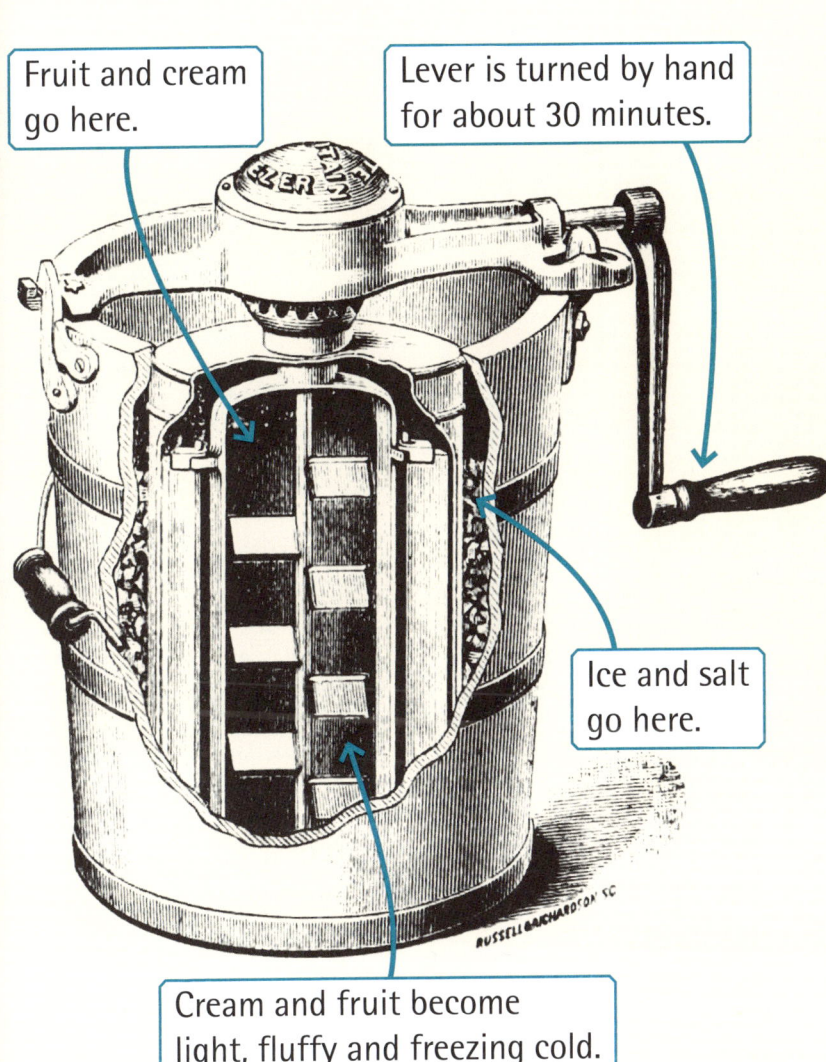

Chapter 2
The code-busting superstar

Games consoles, laptops and mobile phones: all these **devices** can stream content, but have you ever wondered how this works? They use wireless technology like WiFi and Bluetooth.

You might think that such complicated technology must have been developed by huge computer companies in big shiny offices. And often, that's true! Computer companies certainly help to improve WiFi and Bluetooth and make many of the devices that use them. But one of the main ideas behind WiFi and Bluetooth came, perhaps surprisingly, from a film star.

In her lifetime, Hedy Lamarr was best known for acting in films. She was said to be the inspiration for film characters like Catwoman and Disney's Snow White.

Catwoman

Disney's Snow White

And as well as having glitzy outfits and a glamorous lifestyle, Hedy had a brilliant mind.

Inventor fact file

Hedy Lamarr

Year of birth: 1914

Born in: Austria

Invented: frequency hopping

Hedy was born in Vienna, Austria, to Jewish parents. She was originally called Hedwig Kiesler. Her mother was a pianist, and her father was the director of a bank. Hedy's father often took her for long walks where he would talk about different kinds of machines like **trams** or the printing press.

Hedy liked to figure out how things worked. People say that she unscrewed her music box when she was five years old, to understand how it operated!

Hedy, aged 7

If Hedy had been a boy, she would probably have gone on to university and a life of scientific discovery. However, during her childhood around 100 years ago, people thought girls should only do certain things. Hedy took classes in ballet and piano, which were more traditional hobbies for girls than science.

Hedy became an actor at the age of 16. In 1933, while she was still a teenager, she married an older man who insisted that she join him at business meetings. Hedy paid attention. She learnt a lot about technology during the meetings.

In 1937, Hedy left her husband and moved to Hollywood in the US where she quickly became a film star.

But away from the glare of the filmset and red carpet appearances, Hedy still liked to take things apart to understand how they worked.

Hedy had a table at home where she experimented with ideas. In Hollywood, she met the famous inventor Howard Hughes, who was trying to create the fastest airplane in the world. Howard gave Hedy tools so she could keep experimenting in her dressing room while on breaks from acting.

Taking flight

Howard probably didn't expect Hedy to give him advice about airplanes. But still, she shared her thoughts on flight …

"I thought the airplanes were too slow … They shouldn't be square, the wings. So I bought a book of fish, and I bought a book of birds. And then I used the fastest bird and connected it with the fastest fish and then drew it together and showed it to Howard Hughes and he said, 'You're a genius.'"

Experimenting

During Hedy's experiments, she invented a tablet that could be dropped into water to make a flavoured fizzy drink. This invention wasn't a great success. Even Hedy thought the fizzy liquid tasted like medicine!

Then she focused on frequency.

Frequency

Think of the waves of the sea. Some are short and fast; some are long and slow. Radio signals also come in short or fast waves. The number of waves you get in a period of time is called the frequency.

During the Second World War, Hedy wanted to help the US and Britain defeat Nazi Germany.

> The Second World War was a major war that lasted from 1939 to 1945. On one side of the war was Nazi Germany, led by Adolf Hitler, plus Italy and Japan. On the other side were Great Britain and the US, later joined by the Soviet Union (now Russia and some other countries). The war ended when Great Britain's side defeated Nazi Germany's side.

Each side in the war sent secret messages to their armies. They often sent these messages through radio signals. From sitting in on her ex-husband's business meetings years earlier, Hedy knew that was risky. Enemies could listen in on the messages!

Hedy worked with her friend George Antheil to develop "frequency hopping". Instead of sticking with one frequency, a message would "hop" between different frequencies, making it almost impossible for enemies to listen in.

Hedy and George's ideas were ahead of their time. Their invention of frequency hopping was never used during the Second World War. But their ideas paved the way for WiFi and Bluetooth. Frequency hopping keeps the internet safer by making it harder for people to eavesdrop on messages.

Hedy made an important contribution to wireless technology – and proved that there was so much more to her than people saw on film.

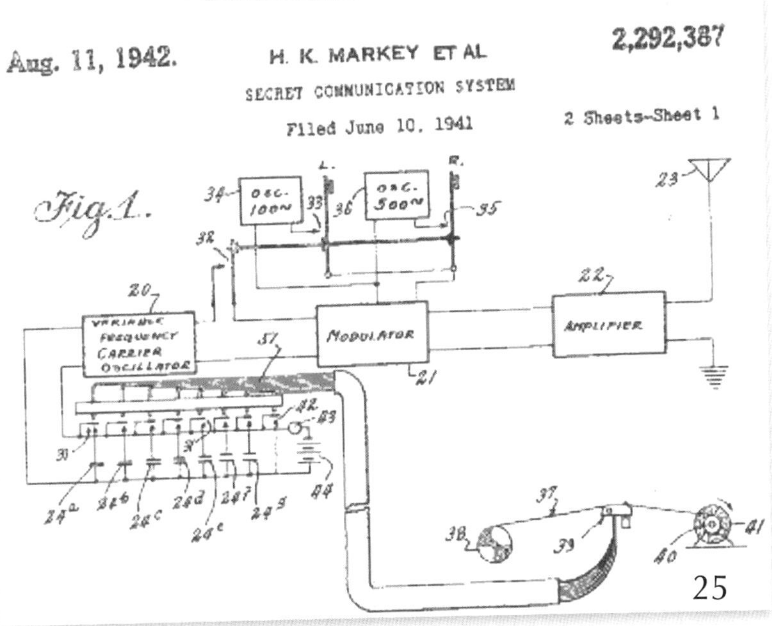

BONUS
Hedy Lamarr, film star and inventor

To most of the world, Hedy Lamarr was a glamorous film star. But she was also an inventor! She was finally added to the National Inventors Hall of Fame in 2014, over 70 years after she helped to invent frequency hopping.

Chapter 3
Bulletproof

Imagine a fabric. It's so light it can be worn as an outfit. It's so strong it can stop bullets. It's so flexible it can be used for race car tyres. That fabric would have to be magical, wouldn't it? Like the cape of a storybook wizard. It can't possibly exist in our own world.

Can it ...?

Inventor fact file

Stephanie Kwolek

Year of birth: 1923

Born in: Pennsylvania, US

Invented: Kevlar

Stephanie Kwolek was born in the state of Pennsylvania in the US on 31st July 1923. That's the same state where, 80 years earlier, Nancy Johnson invented her ice cream machine.

Stephanie's parents were immigrants to the US. They originally came from Poland. Her father worked in a factory, but his passion was nature. In the afternoons, she would join her father to explore the woods and fields near their home. They collected samples of plants and made notes about what they saw. Stephanie kept these in a scrapbook.

Sadly, Stephanie's father died when she was ten years old, and everything changed. Her mother had stayed at home to look after the children, but now she needed to earn money to support the family. Stephanie's mother worked as a seamstress, making and mending clothes on her sewing machine. It was Stephanie's job to care for her brother when she came home from school.

Stephanie's mother loved fashion. Stephanie herself was interested in clothes and thought of working as a fashion designer. But she still had a strong curiosity about science and nature. So instead, she went to university to study chemistry.

Life as a chemist

In 1946, Stephanie finished her university course in chemistry and took a temporary job as a **chemist** at a large company called DuPont. In the 1940s, very few women worked as chemists. Even today, all around the world, men outnumber women in most scientific jobs.

Stephanie didn't come from a wealthy family. She took the job at DuPont because she was hoping to save money so that she could study to be a doctor. Studying to be a doctor took years and it was expensive. But she ended up enjoying her work as a chemist, so she stayed. As part of her job, Stephanie studied types of material like plastic and wood. She tried to figure out their strengths and weaknesses.

In 1965, while she was experimenting with different materials, Stephanie accidentally created a golden, shiny liquid. She was curious. She thought that it might be possible to spin the liquid to make strong **fibres**, and then the fibres could be used to make other things. No one else seemed interested in her strange accident, but she didn't give up. The man in charge of the spinning machine was worried that **particles** in the golden liquid would clog up the machine. But when Stephanie eventually persuaded him to try spinning the liquid, he found that it worked without any problems.

Stronger than steel

"The results came back and they were sort of unbelievable."

Stephanie Kwolek

To Stephanie's delight, she found that when the golden liquid was spun into fibres, the fibres came out incredibly tough. In fact, the substance that she had created was many times stronger than steel. It was also highly **resistant** to heat. The substance was practically fireproof!

You might expect such a tough material to be as heavy as rocks but, in fact, the fibres were very light. Stephanie knew that she'd created something special. In 1971, the material was first sold around the world. It was given the name "Kevlar".

Kevlar fabric

Kevlar doesn't melt or burn at high temperatures – it can resist heat up to almost 430 degrees Celsius. That's over four times greater than the temperature of boiling water!

Kevlar fabric under a microscope

Women in science

Stephanie spent the rest of her working life at DuPont. She always tried to support other women and to help them succeed as chemists. She also spoke at **conferences** where she encouraged young people to become scientists. She went on to win awards for her work, including the US National Medal of Technology.

In 1995, Stephanie was added to the National Inventors Hall of Fame. At the time, she was only the fourth woman to be included.

Stephanie died in 2014 at the age of 90. Today, police officers and other people who work in dangerous situations still wear Kevlar. The strong, tough, lightweight fabric protects them from serious injury.

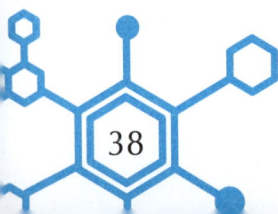

That's why, so many years after the invention of Kevlar, Stephanie's discovery continues to save lives.

"I was fortunate enough to do something that would be a benefit ... I don't think there's anything like saving someone's life to bring you satisfaction and happiness."
Stephanie Kwolek

National Inventors Hall of Fame

BONUS

Kevlar: wonder material

You find it in ...

spacesuits

tyres

skis

bulletproof vests

41

Chapter 4
Fighting disease

A great invention begins with an idea. Maybe it starts with a puzzle you want to solve, or a new way of tackling an old problem. Maybe it strikes you suddenly, like a bolt of lightning out of the blue. But an idea is just the beginning. To be an inventor takes persistence.

> If you have persistence, you continue to do something even though it is difficult.

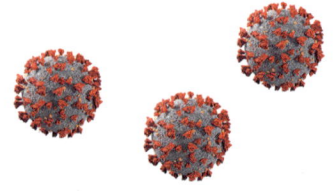

"Sometimes people think you have to be clever to invent. I think most people are quite clever. I think it's the persistence, the perseverance, the ability to deal with failure day in and day out."

Helen Lee

Inventor fact file

Helen Lee

Year of birth: 1940

Born in: China

Invented: disease testing kit "SAMBA"

Helen Lee was born in China. She studied at university in the US and went to work in France. She focused on the different ways that doctors can work out what's making someone ill. For example, doctors can identify broken bones by looking at the injury and taking an X-ray. They also use blood tests to identify lots of diseases.

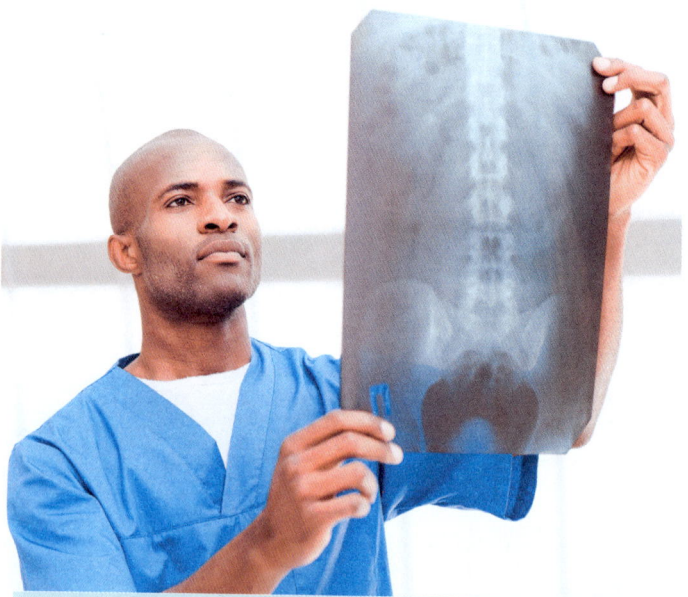

X-rays can show injuries like broken bones.

In a blood test, a doctor or nurse uses a needle to take a small amount of blood from a person's body. The blood is sent to a **laboratory** to be examined. The laboratory will look for things like illnesses, or signs that the person has too little of a particular vitamin.

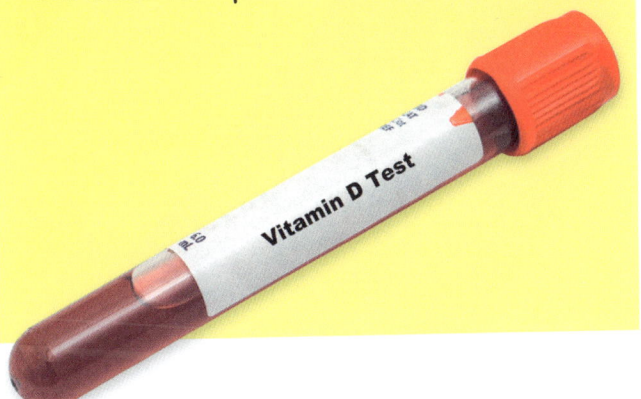

In 1996, when she was in her mid-50s, Helen moved to Cambridge University in the UK. At Cambridge, she studied diseases that affect huge numbers of people around the world.

Helen wanted to help solve the problem of treating diseases in places where it was hard to reach doctors or hospitals. For example, it can be difficult to see a doctor if you live in the countryside in Malawi, a country in the south-east of Africa.

Malawi fact file
- Malawi is landlocked, meaning it has no sea coast. It has a very large lake called Lake Malawi.
- Malawi has two main seasons: the wet season and the dry season. It can get very **humid** in the wet season, and very dusty in the dry season.
- In Malawi a lot of people live in the countryside and work on farms.

Several serious diseases are common in Malawi. People who live in the Malawian countryside often don't know what's making them sick, because there are no doctors near their farms or villages. Even if someone can get to a doctor, it may be hard to get a blood test. You usually need a hospital laboratory to check the results of a blood test. Without these results, you may not get the right medicine.

Trial and error

For years, Helen worked with a team of scientists to invent a blood test that could be used in places like the Malawian countryside.

The test had to be:
- small and light enough to fit on the back of a bike or motorcycle so it could travel all over the countryside
- heatproof and dustproof to survive both the wet and the dry season
- quick and easy to use so it didn't need doctors, nurses or a laboratory in order to get results.

"When you do technology development you fail over and over again."

Helen Lee

It wasn't easy for Helen and her team to develop their blood testing kit. It took five years, and there were lots of problems to solve along the way. At last, after a lot of trial and error, Helen and her team created disease testing kit "SAMBA".

While the work that has gone into SAMBA is far from simple, the kit itself is quick and easy to use. It doesn't need special medical staff, and users can find out the results in less than two hours. SAMBA was made to cope with hot and dusty places, like the countryside in Malawi. But it can also be used to test for other diseases all over the world.

SAMBA is very accurate. As well as identifying a disease, the machine can also detect the amount of virus flowing through a person's bloodstream. This helps medical staff to work out the amount of medicine the patient needs.

Helen won the Popular Prize in the European Inventor Award 2016.

some of the winners of the European Inventor Award 2016

SAMBA II, a new version of the SAMBA disease testing kit, was used at over 100 hospitals to provide rapid test results for the Covid-19 virus. SAMBA II is now being used in the countryside in Malawi, and in other countries where it's difficult to test for diseases.

Helen has proved that a brilliant idea, plus hard work and perseverance, can make a real difference to people's lives.

Helen celebrates winning the Popular Prize.

BONUS

How does SAMBA work?

A sample of blood goes into the machine.

The machine tests the blood and sends the results to a connected tablet.

Chapter 5
Science is for everyone

The study of science and engineering has come on a lot in the last hundred years. More universities have opened around the world, offering science subjects. Experts have carried out research that has changed our understanding of nature, planets and the universe. STEM subjects have never been more popular.

Many inventors started out by studying STEM subjects.

> STEM stands for science, technology, engineering and mathematics.

Science lets us explore the world we live in.

But for much of the 20th century, the world of science and engineering was mostly closed to girls. A lot of people expected girls to look after the home, cooking, cleaning, sewing and mending. Girls were not expected to study at university, particularly not STEM subjects.

The importance of staying curious

For the most part, only boys went to university and became scientists, engineers and inventors – or so a young girl called Valerie Thomas was told when she wanted to study science.

But Valerie didn't agree.

Inventor fact file

Valerie Thomas

Year of birth: 1943

Born in: Maryland, US

Invented: the illusion transmitter

Valerie's father liked to take things apart, such as radios and TVs. He was interested in understanding how they worked. Valerie was interested too. She read lots of books, especially ones about science and technology. At the age of eight, she borrowed a book called *The Boys' First Book of Radio and Electronics*. Valerie hoped that her father would help her with the projects in the book, but he didn't. This left her with the unhappy feeling that electronics was not for girls.

Books and toys based on electronics and problem-solving were once aimed only at boys.

Valerie grew up in the US at a time when many schools separated children based on their skin colour. Her all-girls' school was "integrated", which meant that, unlike some schools, children there were not divided by race. But people still thought that most of the girls would grow up to cook, clean and look after a home, rather than study or work. Valerie was good at maths and curious about science, but no one encouraged her to take an interest in these subjects.

"When I got to high school, there were no classes on electronics, so I sort of gave up. Then, I took a class in physics and it helped to answer the question that I always had: What makes things tick?"

Valerie Thomas

Valerie went to study science at Morgan State University. She was one of only two women in her class to take a type of science called physics as her main subject. She completed her studies in 1964.

Physics is the study of things like light, heat and electricity.

A head for figures

Valerie was good at maths. After university, she got a job as a mathematician at NASA where she worked with computers.

It was while working at NASA in the late 1970s that Valerie came up with her invention, the "illusion transmitter". The illusion transmitter was a way of making flat things look 3D.

NASA scientists study planets, stars and other objects in space.

In 1969, NASA led Apollo 11, the first mission that put people on the moon.

What's the difference between 2D and 3D?

- Two-dimensional or 2D things are flat. You can measure them in length and width but they have no depth. Shapes like triangles, circles, squares and rectangles are 2D.

- Three-dimensional or 3D things look solid. You can measure them in length, width and depth. Shapes like pyramids and cones, spheres, cubes and cuboids are 3D.

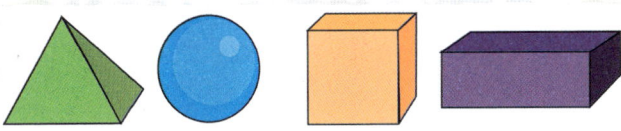

A role model for girls

NASA used Valerie's invention to make 3D pictures of Earth from outer space. This helped people to get a clearer sense of the planet's appearance, and to monitor natural disasters like floods and volcanoes.

Valerie's work has also had an effect outside space science. It's helped to improve the technology that makes 3D films possible. This has led to a new generation of 3D films, like Disney's 3D versions of *The Lion King* and *Beauty and the Beast*. Valerie's work has also led to more 3D experiences, like rides and games that make you feel you are "inside" the story!

Special glasses are used to watch 3D films.

But more than anything, Valerie is proud of her contribution to **diversity** in science.

> "I look back on the things that I have done, I think my biggest legacy is the positive impact that I've had on people."
>
> *Valerie Thomas*

Throughout her career at NASA, Valerie spoke to huge numbers of school children about her work. She encouraged a new generation of young engineers and scientists. In this way, Valerie demonstrated not only a commitment to science, but also to a fairer world.

Science is for everyone.

BONUS

3D films and experiences

People watching a 3D film at a cinema

special glasses for watching 3D films

Here are some 3D films

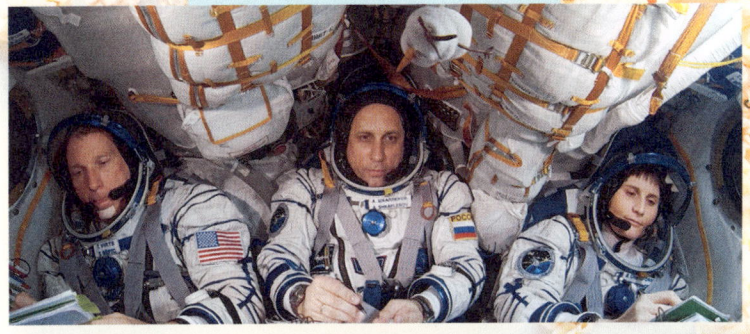

Chapter 6
Turning trash into cash

Over 100 years ago, a scientist called Leo Baekeland created "Bakelite", the first modern plastic. Bakelite was a human-made material that couldn't be found in nature. It only came in dark colours, but that didn't stop it being popular. Bakelite was lightweight and could be moulded into different shapes. It was used to make things like telephones, electrical sockets and light switches.

a Bakelite telephone

a Bakelite light switch

The plastic revolution

Over the years, people developed different types of plastic. These materials were light and tough. They could be melted into almost any shape and could come in every possible colour. Plastic was cheap and easy to make – much cheaper than natural materials like wood. As more and more plastic goods went on sale, plastic became common in homes.

shopping bag

toys

suitcase

The problem with plastic

Modern plastic is incredibly **versatile**. Plastic items can come in practically any shape or size. Plastic can be completely see-through or it can come in any colour.

But plastic also has a major problem: it isn't **biodegradable**.

Plastic bottles can take up to 450 years to break down.

Because plastic doesn't rot, it stays around for a long, long time. Think of all the plastic items that break or are no longer used, like old bath toys, plastic rackets and parts of broken umbrellas. These things usually end up in the bin, where they are collected and thrown into giant rubbish heaps called landfill.

400 million tons of plastic is produced every year. About 40% of this is **single-use plastic**. Plastic waste is a huge issue for the planet. But inventors are seeking solutions to this global problem.

Inventor fact file

Nzambi Matee

Year of birth: 1992

Born in: Kenya

Invented: plastic bricks

Nzambi Matee grew up in Kenya in Eastern Africa. Like Hedy Lamarr and Valerie Thomas, Nzambi wanted to understand what makes things work. She used to take electronic items like radios apart, although she wasn't always sure how to put them back together!

After finishing school, Nzambi studied science at university. During her studies, she learnt about different types of materials like metals and plastics.

After university, Nzambi started to work in an office, but Kenya's plastic problems troubled her. Although Kenya had banned single-use plastics in 2017, the country was littered with plastic waste. Outside the capital city, Nairobi, was a giant rubbish dump, over 120 square metres in size – that's larger than 20 football fields!

Nzambi wanted to use her studies to do something about the problem.

Nzambi set up her own business, Gjenge Makers, in 2017, when she was still in her twenties. She wanted to find a way to reuse plastic waste. She started with a small laboratory in her mother's garden, where she experimented with moulding waste plastic into bricks. After a period of trial and error, Nzambi developed a process for creating rectangular bricks by mixing sand with waste plastic.

"I was like, how can we figure out a way to convert this plastic waste into something useful?"

Nzambi Matee

Nzambi with her sand and waste mix

Gjenge Makers' plastic bricks are a "win-win" solution:

- Companies have to pay to get rid of their waste. Gjenge Makers helps by removing their waste free of charge.

- The waste is used to make plastic bricks for paving. There are plans to make bricks that can be used to build houses too.

- Building materials are expensive. Gjenge Makers' bricks are cheaper than other paving bricks.

- The bricks can be made to different strengths. The toughest are seven times stronger than concrete but a lot lighter.

"I quit my job. I put all my savings into this. I became so broke that everyone thought I was crazy and so many people told me to give up."

Nzambi Matee

But Nzambi didn't give up. Today, Gjenge Makers continues to expand, turning plastic waste into useable bricks. Nzambi has received several awards for her work, including the United Nations Young Champion of the Earth 2020 for Africa and the UK-based Women of the Year Eco-Champion Award 2022.

It all begins with an idea

In this book, we have discovered some amazing inventions and met the women who thought them up. We've seen how one idea can lead to another, like Hedy Lamarr's "frequency hopping", which led to WiFi and Bluetooth, and Valerie Thomas's invention, which led to improvements in 3D films.

There are still so many inventions that haven't been created yet ...

Do you have an idea? Something that will improve our world, make it greener, safer, or simply more delicious?

If you do, take a leaf out of our inventors' book:

✓ Think through your plan.

✓ Do your research.

✓ Ask questions.   (curiosity)

✓ Never give up.

self-belief

(resilience)

perseverance

BONUS

Waste to plastic bricks

Waste plastic is collected from the dump.

The waste is divided into different types of plastic.

The shredded plastic is mixed with sand and coloured.

The plastic mixture is pressed into bricks.

BONUS
Timeline

Nancy Johnson
Year of birth: 1795

Stephanie Kwolek
Year of birth: 1923

Hedy Lamarr
Year of birth: 1914

Helen Lee
Year of birth: 1940

Valerie Thomas
Year of birth: 1943

Nzambi Matee
Year of birth: 1992

Glossary

biodegradable able to be broken down, for example by rotting

chemist a scientist who studies what things are made of

conferences meetings, often of experts like scientists, where people discuss a particular topic

devices pieces of equipment used for particular purposes; games consoles and mobile phones are examples of devices

diversity including a range of people from different backgrounds

fibres thin threads of material, for instance cotton or wool

humid warm, damp weather

laboratory a building where scientific experiments take place

particles very small bits that make up bigger things

resistant capable of stopping or blocking something: for example, if a product is resistant to heat, that means it doesn't melt when it gets hot

single-use plastic plastic items that are only used once, like crisp packets, plastic straws and plastic knives and forks

trams small railway cars, often used inside cities

versatile can be used in many different ways

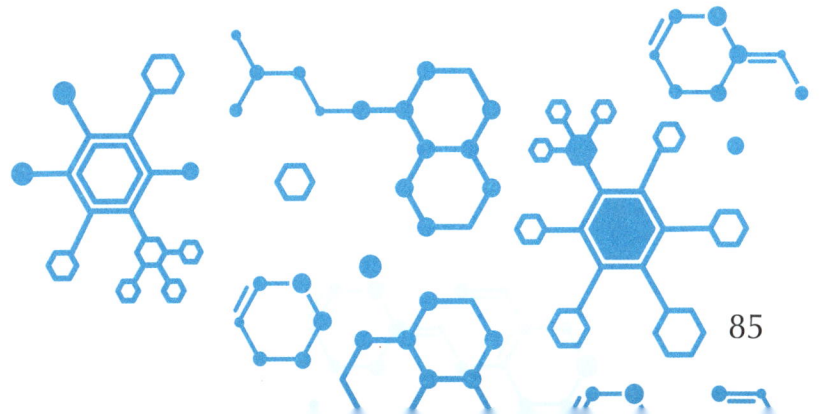

About the author

Why did you decide to become an author?

Inbali Iserles

I always loved stories from the youngest age. On long hot summers when we stayed with my grandparents, my sister and I used to write and illustrate books. My spelling was (and still is) terrible and my handwriting was (and still is) pretty hard to read — but make-believe and storytelling was something I can't remember ever living without!

How did you start your writing career?

I never expected to be an author. I was training to be a lawyer when I came up with the idea for my first book. I couldn't get the idea out of my head so I realised I would have to write the story…

What do you enjoy most about writing?

I love that moment when an idea starts tickling at me, and the thrill of following that idea, wherever it leads.

Which inventor in this book do you admire most?

I'm inspired by all the inventors in this book, but Hedy Lamarr was truly amazing. She spent her whole life being judged on her looks, but she was incredibly intelligent and inventive. Imagine what she might have created if she'd been allowed to pursue a career as an inventor, engineer or scientist?

What would you like to invent?

A time machine. I mean, seriously, how awesome would that be? Think of the possibilities!

If you could meet one of these inventors who would you choose and what would you ask?

That's tricky, as they're all so amazing! Maybe Nzambi Matee, as I'm impressed that she developed an idea and built up a company on her own steam.

I would want to know where she stashes her secret store of resilience — because the ability to keep going when others give up is really at the heart of these stories of inventors.

What is an invention you use every day?

There are so many possible responses to this question, like the computer I'm writing on now as I type out my answer. Perhaps the greatest unsung hero of the modern world is the flushable toilet. You may be surprised to learn that it's still a relatively recent invention!

How can learning about inventors help you in your own life?

Learning about inventors makes us appreciate the technology around us, and inspires us to work harder to create, and to solve problems. Like the inventors in this book, we can learn to work with dedication and perseverance until we achieve our goals!

Book chat

When you saw the cover, what did you think this book would be about? Were you right?

Had you heard of any of these people or inventions before reading this book?

What was the most interesting thing you learnt from this book?

Have you read any books like this before?

Was anything in this book particularly surprising?

If you had to think of a new title for the book, what would you choose?

If you could talk to any of the inventors in this book, who would you pick and what would you ask?

Can you think of an invention you use everyday?

Can you think of any inventors who aren't in this book?

Who would you recommend this book to and why?

What do you think is the best invention ever and why?

Which invention from the book do you think is best and why?

Do you have a favourite inventor?

Would you like to be an inventor? Why or why not?

Book challenge:

Draw a diagram of your very own invention.

Published by Collins An imprint of HarperCollins*Publishers*

The News Building
1 London Bridge Street
London
SE1 9GF
UK

Macken House
39/40 Mayor Street Upper
Dublin 1
D01 C9W8
Ireland

Text © Inbali Iserles 2025

Design and illustrations © HarperCollins*Publishers* Limited 2025

Inbali Iserles asserts her moral right to be identified as author of this work.

10 9 8 7 6 5 4 3 2 1

ISBN 978-0-00-874645-2

All rights reserved. No part of this publication may be reproduced, stored in a retrieval system, or transmitted in any form by any means, electronic, mechanical, photocopying, recording or otherwise, without the prior written permission of the Publisher or a licence permitting restricted copying in the United Kingdom issued by the Copyright Licensing Agency Ltd, 5th Floor, Shackleton House, 4 Battle Bridge Lane, London SE1 2HX.

Without limiting the author's and publisher's exclusive rights, any unauthorised use of this publication to train generative artificial intelligence (AI) technologies is expressly prohibited. HarperCollins also exercise their rights under Article 4(3) of the Digital Single Market Directive 2019/790 and expressly reserve this publication from the text and data mining exception.

British Library Cataloguing-in-Publication Data
A catalogue record for this publication is available from the British Library.

Download the teaching notes and word cards to accompany this book at:
http://littlewandle.org.uk/signupfluency/

Get the latest Collins Big Cat news at
collins.co.uk/collinsbigcat

Author: Inbali Iserles
Publisher: Laura White
Product managers: Caroline Green and Holly Woolnough
Series editor: Charlotte Raby
Development editor: Catherine Baker
Commissioning editor: Caroline Green
Project manager: Emily Hooton
Copyeditor: Sally Byford
Proofreader: Catherine Dakin
Cover designer: Sarah Finan
Typesetter: 2Hoots Publishing Services Ltd
Production controller: Katharine Willard
Printed in the UK.

MIX
Paper | Supporting responsible forestry
FSC™ C007454

This book contains FSC™ certified paper and other controlled sources to ensure responsible forest management.

For more information visit: www.harpercollins.co.uk/green

Made with responsibly sourced paper and vegetable ink

Scan to see how we are reducing our environmental impact.

Acknowledgements
The publishers gratefully acknowledge the permission granted to reproduce the copyright material in this book. Every effort has been made to trace copyright holders and to obtain their permission for the use of copyright material. The publishers will gladly receive any information enabling them to rectify any error or omission at the first opportunity.

Front cover Plastic Ghost/Shutterstock & Kristina Tutanova/Shutterstock, p2l ARCHIVIO GBB/Alamy, p2r Pictorial Press Ltd/Alamy, p3 & 82tl Library of Congress, Washington, D.C. (LC-DIG-ppmsca-54216), p7 & 82cl United States Patent and Trademark Office, p9 Lambert/Getty Images, p12 DeAgostini/Getty Images, p13 Reading Room 2020/Alamy, p15l Everett Collection Inc/Alamy, p15r Moviestore Collection Ltd/Alamy, p16 & 82bl Silver Screen Collection/Hulton Archive/Getty Images, p17 Everett Collection Inc/Alamy, p18 Associated Press/Alamy, p19 PictureLux/The Hollywood Archive/Alamy, p21t Everett Collection Inc/Alamy, pp22–23 (background) edwardolive/Shutterstock, p25t Photo by Joe Petrella/NY Daily News Archive via Getty Images, p25b & 82br Pictorial Press Ltd/Alamy, p26tl Album/Alamy, p26tr Edward Roth/Alamy, p26bl Pictorial Press Ltd/Alamy, p26br Allstar Picture Library Ltd/Alamy, p27tl Cinematic/Alamy, p27tr PictureLux/The Hollywood Archive/Alamy, p27bl Cinematic/Alamy, p27br Shawshots/Alamy, p28 & 82tr Photo12/TopFoto, p32 Pictorial Press Ltd/Alamy, p35 Associated Press/Alamy, p37t Phil Degginger/Science Photo Library, p37b & 82tr Sinclair Stammers/Science Photo Library, p39 Jon Bilous/Alamy, p41b & 78tr Artur Nychyporenko/Alamy, p43 & 83tl European Patent Office, p51 European Patent Office, p52 European Patent Office, p53 European Patent Office, p54b European Patent Office, pp55t, 78bl & 83cl European Patent Office, p55b European Patent Office, p58 & 83tr NASA/Interim Archives/Getty Images, p59 My Childhood Memories/Alamy, p66t Imaginechina Limited/Alamy, p66c Basement Stock/Alamy, p67t TCD/Prod.DB/Alamy, p67tc Lifestyle pictures/Alamy, p67bc TCD/Prod.DB/Alamy, p72 & 83bl Dave Benett/Getty Images for Women of the Year, p75 Simon Maina/AFP/Getty Images, p76 & 83br Simon Maina/AFP/Getty Images, p77 Dave Benett/Getty Images for Women of the Year, p78br Simon Maina/AFP/Getty Images, p80b Simon Maina/AFP/Getty Images, p81t Simon Maina/AFP/Getty Images, p81b Simon Maina/AFP/Getty Images, back cover t European Patent Office, bl Simon Maina/AFP/Getty Images, br Associated Press/Alamy.
All other photos Shutterstock.